The Last Petal Falls

Bianca Budwin

BookLeaf Publishing

India | USA | UK

Presentation by *BookLeaf Publishing*

Web: www.bookleafpub.com

E-mail: info@bookleafpub.com

ISBN: 9789357446358

First edition 2022

In Love

He's just a boy and she's just a girl. Both so young, both so in love.
When they see each other it's like a warm cozy feeling.
Like drinking hot cocoa near the fire as snow is falling on the ground. People called it puppy love, they call it in love.

Fell In Love

Falling in love with their touch.
Fell in love with the way their lips felt up
against yours.
Fell in love with the way they run their fingers
through your hair.
Fell in love with the way they say your name.
Fell in love with the overwhelming feeling of
happiness.
Fell in love with just them.

Addiction

When so many people hear that word they
immediately think of drugs and alcohol.
Which simply isn't the case,
You can be addicted to people!
You know the wrong type of people.
The people your family always tells you to look
out for, simply like a lion hunting its prey.
You get a little bit of attention from someone
who isn't the right person for you, so you're
fiening off of this adrenaline running through
your body and lighting up every single cell in
you.
Of trying to get it one last time.
Which can lead to bad behavior, and bad habits.
When you don't have it, you get this empty
feeling of something that you need, you want.

Joyful

Being around you makes me so joyful. As if we're laying in a field of flowers with the sun shining on us with a nice cool breeze. Being so thankful that I have you in my life. As time winds it reoccurs how valuable you are in my life.

Love

What can I say. But just happiness and positivity. Butterflies in my stomach every time I see you, when your lips touched mine it seem like that's where they were always supposed to be. My mom telling me that love makes people crazy and blindsided. I brushed her off like she didn't know what she was talking about, but did she see something I couldn't? That first lie you told, even if it was a little one, but you loved me so it was okay, right?
Love, what can I say. You make me feel like I'm the only girl in this world. But too scared to tell anyone about us, but you love me so it's okay, right? Maybe I was too blindsided to know you ever ashamed of me. That little lie you told, making me feel crazy. How I believe you, and when I didn't, you shut me out and turn it back on you. As if you were the victim. When you says that you're not like everyone else, silly me for believing you. But you love me so it's okay, right? All the love and respect I had for myself is gone, because you loved me right?
Love, it's a funny word, please don't use it if you don't mean it!

Beauty

Beauty has nothing to do with just about your outer looks, you have to have inner beauty to have outer beauty. Don't doubt your outer beauty with flaws by staring at yourself in the mirror thinking you should look a type away because society says what's beautiful and what's not. Everybody is their own image like somebody painted you on a canvas and are so proud of what they see and if you pick out every little thing you're criticizing the artist who painted you. If you have stretch marks on your stomach or on your thighs take it as you are a beautiful tiger expressing the beauty in which you are!

Tears

When that first tear drop hits your sleeve,
Looking in your eyes seeing all the pain you
were trying to hide.
Don't you know that the eyes are the windows to
the soul?
Looking in your eyes as they're starting to water,
You were trying to put on a brave face as tears
are running down your cheek.
Trying to hold back the pain beneath the surface.

Night-Time

Seeing all the twinkling lights in the sky with
you,
Looking through your sunroof.
Even though it's dark I'm safe with you as I'm
analyzing your eyes, holding your hand, taking a
deep breath.
As the night goes on listening to music and
making wishes to the stars with you

Kisses

As your top lip and bottom lip touch to give me
a kiss on the cheek. It's so soft and sweet.
Or when your lips touch mine, feeling like that's
where they were always meant to be every time
our lips touch having fireworks explode like it's
the Fourth of July.
Adrenaline running through my body, so joyful
and excited. Electricity in the air, all just by your
kisses.

Change

Life goes on and things change. The one thing I know for sure is my feelings toward you will never change, you came in my life and flipped it completely upside down had me doing a 360. You comforted me when things were changing in my life, when everything was unfamiliar but you. You showed me that change is the possibility of anything. I don't want any possibility to change if it is with you.

Turtle In The Blue Sea

On October 24 I was born.
Meeting the rest of my brothers and sisters.
I can taste the sea salt, smell the ocean, hear the
waves hitting the rocks.
We all head straight to the oceans.
As the first wave hit me,
I almost tumbled over.
As I make it into the blue sea,
It's bigger than I ever imagined.
All the beautiful animals in the sea.
One week into the blue sea,
I see a lot of abnormal things.
There is a lot of trash in the ocean,
I got my fin stuck in a plastic bag.
There was a plastic straw in my nose.
It's extremely painful.
I don't know how to get it out.
One month into the blue sea,
The water is getting warmer.
I can see the water covering what used to be
land.
I decided to go on the land,

All these people are coming around me.
Fear ran through my body
My heart beating through my chest.
They came towards me with a sharp object.
I didn't know what they were about to do with
me.
The fear started to go away,
 Once I knew that they were trying to help me
and not harm me.
They got the plastic straw out of my nostril,
And I feel a lot better.
They let me back in the ocean.
2 days later,
I saw something else happen to one of my
brothers.
He got caught in a soda ring.
I can see that I was one of the lucky ones,
I got help from amazing people.
I wish trash wouldn't be in the ocean,
So we can swim around freely without getting
caught in something.

Loneliness

You know that feeling when you're lying in bed.
Just staring at your ceiling. Having one thousand
thoughts running through your mind and only
sixty seconds.
That weight on your chest,
It feels like an elephant just sitting on top of you.
The feeling of not being able to breathe, wanting
to scream, but nothing comes out.
Loneliness.
Having people around you, no one to relate to.
Wanting to tell someone how you feel, but not
put pressure on them. Not to worry about what
you're going through because they have their
own shit to deal with too.
Or that's at least what you tell yourself, right…
Those lonely nights just creeping up towards
you, crying yourself to sleep l, shhh.. don't
wanna be too loud. You won't want anyone to
hear your whimper of cries.
Loneliness.

Lose

Having all this feeling and emotional, that you just don't know what to do with them.
Can make you lose yourself. Losing yourself to see the greater good in people.
Sticking around to see if they will treat you right, hoping that one day you'll be treated with respect and honesty that you deserve.
But as you wait, you stop thinking about yourself, and you start to lose your morals and the respect you have for yourself.

Risks

I laid my heart on the line for you, risking my emotions and broken self for you. Risk getting my heart broken again, hoping you're different from everyone else. Nowadays people just want a hookup, but that's not what I'm looking for. Risking my time and energy hoping you are different, praying that you are the one.

Upset

That feeling that you and only you alone can
feel.
When you sit there so mad at the world,
So mad at yourself that you have no explanation
for anything.
Feeling so defenseless and helpless that you ball
it all up until it's just like a grenade about to
explode. You can't help but wonder why you
feel so angry and upset towards everything,
Wanting to explode what is wrong.
But you don't even know.

Insecurities

I'm looking at myself in the mirror,
Trying to visualize what I want to see.
People telling me how beautiful I am,
I wish I could believe them I wish I could see
you myself the way they see me.
Wishing I looked a certain way.
My insecurities build so high that it's like a brick
wall trying to climb.
Every scratch on my palm is an insult I get to
myself, Every scrape on my knee is me beating
myself up with the negativity.

Just A Broken Girl

I gave you my whole heart, thinking I would receive yours in return. I would've never heard it, but I can see that the feelings weren't reciprocated. After all the emotions I put in and telling you how scared I would be to get hurt again. Feelings weren't reciprocated. I watched you take my heart and crush it into a thousand pieces like it was nothing, like it didn't mean anything. When you told me you would not hurt me, I should've known that I was just your prey. Jokes on me, huh? Now I'm just a broken girl!

Rose

She is a rose,
Starting to blossom. . .
Her petals are trying to touch the sun.
So delicate and fragile.
Someone coming along thinking it to be cute
and funny.
To pick her petals one by one.
Until there's nothing left.
Leaving her destroyed and broken,
For someone else to clean up.
Having all her petals scattered all over the
ground like she was nothing.
As if the wind is blowing her farther and farther
too far that you can no longer see her…
She is a rose fragile and delicate.
She tries to bloom,
Stretching too far,
The last petal falls.